THE ONE PLACE WE ALL CALL HOME

First published in the United Kingdom in hardback
by HarperCollins *Children's Books* in 2019
First published in paperback in 2023
HarperCollins *Children's Books* is a division of HarperCollins*Publishers* Ltd
1 London Bridge Street, London SE1 9GF

www.harpercollins.co.uk

HarperCollins*Publishers*
1st Floor, Watermarque Building, Ringsend Road, Dublin 4, Ireland

1 3 5 7 9 10 8 6 4 2

Text copyright © Matt Whyman 2019
Cover and interior illustrations copyright © Richard Jones 2019
Foreword copyright © David Attenborough 2019
See page 93 for copyright details of all photographs.
Cover design copyright © HarperCollins*Publishers* Ltd 2019
Netflix is a trademark of Netflix, Inc.
Artwork used with permission of Netflix Studios, LLC
© 1986 Panda Symbol WWF – World Wide Fund For Nature
(Formerly World Wildlife Fund)
® "WWF" is a WWF Registered Trademark
All rights reserved.

ISBN 978-0-00-856060-7

Matt Whyman and Richard Jones assert the moral right to be
identified as the author and illustrator of the work respectively.
A CIP catalogue record for this title is available from the
British Library.

Printed in Italy

Conditions of Sale: This book is sold subject to the
condition that it shall not, by way of trade or otherwise,
be lent, re-sold, hired out or otherwise circulated without
the publisher's prior consent in any form, binding or
cover other than that in which it is published and
without a similar condition including this condition
being imposed on the subsequent purchaser.

MIX
Paper | Supporting
responsible forestry
FSC™ C007454

This book is produced from independently certified FSC™ paper
to ensure responsible forest management.

For more information visit: www.harpercollins.co.uk/green

OUR PLANET

THE ONE PLACE WE ALL CALL HOME

Foreword by David Attenborough

Written by Matt Whyman

Illustrations by Richard Jones

Executive Consultant Editor Colin Butfield

HarperCollins *Children's Books*

Contents

Foreword by David Attenborough 8
A Map of Our Planet 10
One Planet 12

Our Frozen Worlds 14
   All About Our Frozen Worlds 16
   Stories From Our Frozen Worlds 18
   Protecting Our Frozen Worlds 22

Our Jungles 24
   All About Our Jungles 26
   Stories From Our Jungles 28
   Protecting Our Jungles 32

Our Coastal Seas 34
   All About Our Coastal Seas 36
   Stories From Our Coastal Seas 38
   Protecting Our Coastal Seas 42

Our Deserts & Grasslands 44
   All About Our Deserts & Grasslands 46
   Stories From Our Deserts & Grasslands 48
   Protecting Our Deserts & Grasslands 52

Our High Seas 54
   All About Our High Seas 56
   Stories From Our High Seas 58
   Protecting Our High Seas 62

Our Fresh Water 64
   All About Our Fresh Water 66
   Stories From Our Fresh Water 68
   Protecting Our Fresh Water 72

Our Forests 74
   All About Our Forests 76
   Stories From Our Forests 78
   Protecting Our Forests 82

One Chance 84
One Future 85
Our Amazing Planet 86
Glossary 88
Index 90
Photo Credits 93
Acknowledgements 93

Foreword

Nature is full of thrilling stories. Some tell how certain animals manage to live in even the harshest places on Earth. What could be more astonishing — and appalling — than the way male emperor penguins spend almost half of every year standing in total darkness, lashed by ferocious, freezing blizzards, with nothing whatsoever to eat. Other creatures seem to be living in luxury. Orangutans clambering around in the forests of Borneo are surrounded by all kinds of fruit. The problem is that while some fruits are rich and nutritious, others are extremely poisonous. So a mother has to spend years carefully teaching her baby to know which is which.

Some of these tales are about travel. Salmon, having spent the early years of their lives feeding in the ocean, somehow or other manage to find the mouth of the exact river in which they were hatched, and then swim right up to its shallow headwaters in order to lay their own eggs in exactly the same place. There are other stories of chase and escape. Polar bears have astonishing techniques of stalking seals that rest out on the ice. They have to move extremely slowly, with inexhaustible patience and only when they believe the seal is not looking at them, until at last they are close enough to pounce. Cheetahs, on the other hand, catch antelope by chasing them across the open grassy plains of Africa and reach speeds faster than those achieved by anything else on four legs.

Human beings also appear in these stories. Only too often, however, they seem to be the villains, for the truth is that we have not treated the world with the care that we should have done. But that is not so in all the stories. One relates how we, almost without realising what we were doing, very nearly exterminated a species. When I was a boy, human beings hunted whales so mercilessly, and so successfully, that they were brought close to extinction. Fortunately, that story has a happy ending. Just in time, the seafaring nations of the world joined together and agreed to stop the slaughter, and now there are more whales in the oceans than at any time within living memory.

So here they are — tales of travel, detective stories, domestic dramas and much else. Some we have known since the beginnings of human history when we lived by hunting. Others we have only just started to understand. And be prepared to add your own, because you will be among the next characters who can, if they wish, tell the most extraordinary story of all — how human beings in the twenty-first century came to their senses and started to protect Planet Earth and all the other wonderful forms of life with which we share it.

David Attenborough

A blue whale dives to feed in the Gulf of California

A Map of Our Planet
OUR DIFFERENT HABITATS

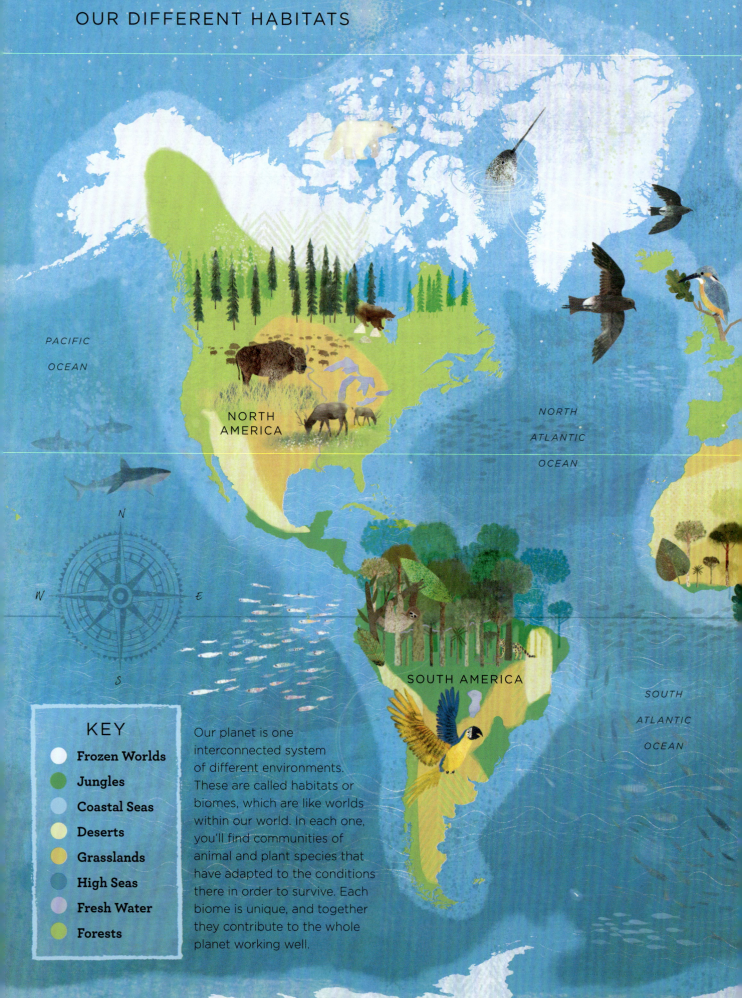

KEY
- Frozen Worlds
- Jungles
- Coastal Seas
- Deserts
- Grasslands
- High Seas
- Fresh Water
- Forests

Our planet is one interconnected system of different environments. These are called habitats or biomes, which are like worlds within our world. In each one, you'll find communities of animal and plant species that have adapted to the conditions there in order to survive. Each biome is unique, and together they contribute to the whole planet working well.

One Planet

The different habitats that make up our planet might seem to be completely distinct and separate worlds, but, in fact, they are closely linked. From the high seas to the shallow waters around our coastlines, the forests and jungles to grasslands and deserts, freshwater environments to the ice worlds at the top and bottom of our planet, an astonishing diversity of life on Earth depends on these global connections.

American bison in Yellowstone National Park

Our Frozen Worlds

Located at the top and bottom of the globe, the poles represent some of the Earth's last remaining wildernesses. We are only just beginning to fully understand these extraordinary places, and yet they are undergoing changes that affect us all.

A polar bear stalks the ice in the Arctic

Our Frozen Worlds

ALL ABOUT
Our Frozen Worlds

The ice world of Antarctica that surrounds the south pole has been frozen for thirty million years. It is bigger than Europe, and it's the coldest and windiest place on Earth.

Here, entire mountain ranges are buried under ice up to four kilometres thick. Each winter, even large areas of the vast Southern Ocean that surround it freeze. It may look as if no life can exist here, but under the sea ice is a world teeming with activity.

The Antarctic waters are full of nutrients that feed plankton, which makes up the bottom of the food chain. Plankton is eaten by tiny shrimp-like creatures called krill, which in turn are eaten by seals, penguins, seabirds and whales.

The northern ice cap of our planet is called the Arctic. This is a frozen ocean ringed by land.

Sea ice supports a wide range of species, from microscopic algae to walruses, as well as huge flocks of migrating seabirds. Then there are the narwhals, sporting tusks like unicorns of the icy seas, and, of course, there's the world's largest land carnivore, the polar bear.

At both poles, ice has been a feature for millions of years. Now things are changing. This is because of human activity, and, in particular, our use of fossil fuels, such as oil, natural gas and coal. Burning fossil fuels releases carbon dioxide into the Earth's atmosphere. This is causing the planet to warm up, and it is melting the polar ice.

As a result of rising temperatures, we are losing ice at a rate that's having a big impact on wildlife in the Arctic and the Antarctic.

Special Quality

Ice is a special feature of the poles. Animals from penguins to seals to polar bears need ice platforms to help them hunt, rest and breed.

The poles might seem like a world away, but they affect all our lives and it's essential they stay frozen to lock in water that would otherwise cause sea levels to rise, as well as to reflect the sun's rays back into space to keep our planet from overheating.

Our Frozen Worlds

Penguins resting on an iceberg in Antarctica

STORIES FROM
Our Frozen Worlds
POP-UP PENGUIN

In South Georgia, a king penguin pops up on to the shore, having surfaced from the water at speed. It's a smart move as a leopard seal has been lurking, ready to strike. The penguin has been diving for fish to feed his chick. Now he needs to find the youngster amid a penguin colony that stretches around the bay.

While the leopard seal watches hungrily from the water, the penguin faces another challenge in getting back to his chick. He has to dodge two male elephant seals that are scrapping over a female on the shore. This means moving quickly to avoid being bulldozed by four tonnes of angry blubber. Once he's reached the colony, which contains half a million chicks, the penguin calls and listens for a recognisable cry. Astonishingly, despite the racket, he can recognise his little one's response. The things parents go through to feed the family!

King penguin leaps ashore

Our Frozen Worlds

King penguin calling for his chick

ARCTIC CHASE

A polar bear and her cub stalk the Arctic sea ice in search of a seal. Recently, the sea has been freezing later than usual. As a result, the winter storms that would usually bash up the surface and create ridges in the ice have passed. It means the surface of this stretch of frozen Arctic water is almost completely flat. There are no places to hide, and this makes it challenging for the bears to creep up on their supper.

For the seal, these new conditions also make life difficult. A mother seal would normally use the frozen ridges to create a den for her pup.

With nowhere to hide now, all she can do is hope her young one quickly learns to keep an eye out. This time, the bear cub has yet to learn to tread as softly as her mother. Picking up on the bears' approach, the seal pup slips through a hole in the ice and into the safety of the sea.

Without doubt, life is changing for the likes of the polar bear and the seal. Fewer hiding places in the ice mean both predator and prey must adapt to survive, but a warming climate means things can only become tougher.

New threat to Antarctic whales

Humpback whale numbers have recovered dramatically since the ban on commercial whaling, but now their food supply is under threat due to climate change. The amount of Antarctic krill, on which they rely, has halved in the last fifty years, partly due to warming temperatures and melting sea ice.

Polar bears and seal

PLANET KRILL

In the cold Southern Ocean around Antarctica, most marine life, from penguins to seals to humpback whales, depends on krill. These tiny crustaceans — like miniature shrimp — feed on phytoplankton (see page 60), and so they form an essential link in the food chain. There are estimated to be 780 trillion krill in the world's oceans, and altogether they weigh more than the total human population. But due to climate change their numbers are shrinking.

BIG BIRD

The wandering albatross chick can spend up to a year in the nest. While its parents take off far across the water, wandering the Southern Ocean in search of food, this rather large little one often waits for up to a week between meals.

ICE GIANTS

The walrus is about the same size and weight as a family car. Insulated by thick layers of blubber that can withstand temperatures of -35°C, this hefty Arctic beast feeds mostly on molluscs such as clams as well as on other marine animals, including shrimp, crabs and occasionally seals. The ice provides the walrus with both a platform from which to dive for food and a place to sleep and mate, but as climate change causes the ice to shrink, huge numbers of them are forced to gather on coastlines. With limited space, often far from their feeding grounds, many do not survive.

ORCA V. PENGUIN

The orca, also known as the killer whale, is a fearsome hunter. It's classed as an apex predator, which means it is at the top of the food chain and isn't preyed upon by any other creature in nature. Over half the world's orca population can be found in the Antarctic's waters. Orcas often hunt in packs, or pods, and shift into a stealth mode so they move quickly and quietly through the water to target their prey. Penguins are quick enough to outmanoeuvre a single orca, but they are no match for a pod.

PROTECTING
Our Frozen Worlds

The north and south poles contain masses of water **LOCKED UP AS ICE.** This helps keep sea levels from rising and flooding coastal regions.

Polar ice **PROTECTS** the planet. It locks up carbon, which is linked to climate change, and reflects the sun's rays back into space.

THE HEAT IS ON . . .
Burning fossil fuels is causing global temperatures to rise. As the polar ice shrinks, it doesn't just affect the wildlife that depends on it but the world as a whole.

GO CLEAN, STAY COOL.
We have the technology to slow rising temperatures by switching to clean and **RENEWABLE ENERGY** sources such as wind and solar power. That's good for our ice worlds, and the **FUTURE** of the Earth.

Our Jungles

Home to a staggering range of species, many still undiscovered, jungles are among the oldest and most diverse ecosystems on Earth. They are precious spaces that play a vital role in the health of our planet, and yet their future is far from safe.

A lowland gorilla cub takes a ride in the Congo jungle, Africa

Our Jungles

Giant jungle

The largest jungle on Earth can be found in South America's Amazon basin. This vast natural kingdom is ten times the size of France, and home to one tenth of the world's animal species.

Life at all levels in the Amazon jungle

ALL ABOUT
Our Jungles

Jungles are forests where it is warm all the time and rains almost every day. They are found on or near the equator, which is an imaginary line round the middle of the planet, and stretch from the Amazon in South America to the Congo in Africa, and across to Southeast Asia and the Pacific Islands. Jungles are lush, green habitats where the constant warmth and wetness mean nature is incredibly active.

Jungles support life at all levels, from within the soil to the uppermost tree branches. Each jungle, or even small corner of a jungle, can contain a unique cast of species found nowhere else on Earth.

Many jungle plants and animals have developed particular relationships that mean they depend on each other for their survival. In equatorial Africa, for instance, the western lowland gorilla is responsible for spreading seeds from a fruit it likes to eat. This is because the seeds survive the gorilla's digestion and are found in its dung. In South America, the Amazon's towering Brazil-nut tree relies on the sharp teeth of the agouti, a jungle rodent that cracks open its pods to free the seeds. The jungle is home to all manner of strange and remarkable relationships. Leafcutter ants carry leaves into their colonies to grow fungus on for food. Then there is the strangler fig that grows by winding round a host tree and slowly killing it.

Special Quality

Diversity is a special feature of jungles. This means that there is an enormous range of different species, all closely reliant on each other for survival.

Orangutans swinging in the treetops

STORIES FROM
Our Jungles
A HOME FOR EDEN

In the swamp forests of northern Sumatra, Indonesia, an orangutan is teaching her young one how to swing between trees. Field scientists working to protect the species in this area have called the little orangutan Eden. By the time Eden turns ten and becomes an adult, he will need to know how to survive on his own. He watches his mother closely, slowly learning everything about his jungle environment. Without her, this little orangutan could not survive.

It's going to take a long time for Eden to learn where to find the trees that give the best fruit, or how to use a stick to pick out insects from their hiding places.

As he grows up, he'll need to map out everything in his head, which is why scientists are worried about the damaging effect of human activity on his home.

Orangutans need forests to live in, but sadly here in Sumatra more than half of these forests have been destroyed in just a few decades. This is where the jungle is cut down for timber or to make way for roads, housing or farming, especially palm oil plantations. Palm oil is cheap to make, but it comes at a high price.

We lose one hundred orangutans a week due to human actions, including deforestation and hunting. There is still hope for Eden and his kind but their future rests with us.

What is palm oil?

It's a cheap, nutritious vegetable oil used in many food products — bread, spreads, ice cream — and also many cosmetics. Look out for it in the products you buy and use every day, and choose products made with sustainable deforestation-free palm oil or ask companies to change the palm oil they buy to one grown in a way that protects rainforests.

Palm oil plantations

Palm oil itself is not necessarily bad — clearing jungles to grow it is the problem. Hundreds and hundreds of hectares covered in just this one plant replace the jungle that used to support an amazing variety of life. Orangutans' homes are destroyed and enormous numbers of other species are lost. We need to grow palm oil without chopping down more trees.

Our Jungles

Young orangutan

ZOMBIE ANTS

Deep inside the Amazon basin, the world's largest tropical jungle, a carpenter ant is behaving strangely. This one had been crossing the forest floor in search of fresh leaves. Now it has begun to climb a plant as if something inside it is controlling its movements. Amazingly, that is exactly what is happening.

Eventually, this zombie ant will be forced to bite down on a leaf, and then it will die. But that isn't the end of the story, for soon after, alien-like shoots will sprout from its head. This is a killer fungus called *Ophiocordyceps*. The alien shoot holds the fungus's pod of spores, which will drift to the ground, and come into contact with another unsuspecting ant victim — and the cycle will begin again.

Life in the jungle might seem brutal at times, but this gruesome story is part of the jungle's way of keeping itself healthy! The fungus infects the most common species and this means that no single species' population can grow too big or take over. It's one of nature's ways of keeping things balanced and protecting this incredible ecosystem.

Jungle mini-worlds

Each tiny patch of jungle has its own unique world of species — if we destroy even a small area, we are destroying a strand of the intricate web of life.

HIGH FLYER

The Bornean clouded leopard is the biggest predator in Malaysian Borneo. As well as prowling across the forest floor, it sometimes climbs up into the tree canopy to hunt for monkeys.

MIGHTY EAGLE

Over 90 per cent of the tropical rainforest has disappeared from the Philippine islands. What's left is the last refuge for one of the world's rarest birds of prey, with just 400 pairs remaining. The mighty Philippine eagle was once known as the monkey-eating eagle, but it will hunt everything from bats to squirrels, to snakes and even deer.

TIDY-UP TIME

Each male bird of paradise has a special display for attracting mates. Before the western parotia performs his dance, he spends time carefully sweeping leaves and jungle debris from a clearing. Once his stage is ready, the courting can begin. In his elaborate dance he bows, whirls, shuffles and flashes a colourful throat patch.

PROTECTING
Our Jungles

Jungles and other forests are the **LUNGS OF OUR PLANET.** They improve the quality of the air by absorbing carbon dioxide and giving out **OXYGEN.** We cannot afford to keep cutting them down.

We rely on jungles to help **WATER** the world. These green spaces help to **CONTROL OUR CLIMATE** by soaking up vast amounts of water. When this evaporates back into the atmosphere, it's often carried to drier regions that **NEED IT MOST.**

There is no need to clear more jungle. With careful management, we can **REUSE LAND** to produce everything we need from these regions.

SHOP SMART.
We can help by checking labels on our products to be sure they come from sources that **PROTECT** our jungles and the wildlife within them as well as local communities. Even palm-oil products can be sustainable, but it's down to us to **CHOOSE** them.

Our Coastal Seas

In the ocean waters that fringe our lands, rich communities of marine life work together in a way that's vital to the health of our planet and humanity. The coastal seas also provide us with a plentiful supply of food to eat, but only if we work with this environment and not against it.

A green turtle glides over the reefs of Heron Island, Great Barrier Reef

Our Coastal Seas

Grey reef sharks

Special Quality

Coastal seas are all about **abundance**, where members of living communities thrive in huge numbers.

ALL ABOUT
Our Coastal Seas

The waters around our coasts make up less than a tenth of the world's oceans, yet, astonishingly, they are home to an estimated 90 per cent of all marine creatures. Sunlight powers the ecosystem here due to the shallow water, which means that plants can grow. These provide food for lots of different species, and a safe place for many to thrive, breed and raise their young.

The coastal seas are made up of many different ecosystems. These include estuaries, lagoons, rock pools, salt marshes, mangrove forests and fields of underwater seagrasses. Then there are coral reefs, which are where a quarter of all marine life can be found, from microscopic plants to large monk seals and manta rays.

Each ecosystem contains a close-working community of species dependent on one another to keep the food web going. There is a huge range of living things: crabs, limpets, seabirds, sponges and hundreds of types of fish — including sharks. If one species struggles because of changes to the environment, then it can cause big problems. Predators may suffer from a shortage of prey, for example, while other populations can grow too large without hunters and then use up precious resources.

Coastal seas are also critically important to our way of life. Around the world, billions of people rely on fishing for their main source of protein, or for an income. While these waters can provide us with all the fish we need, if we take too much, this affects the whole ecosystem.

Red rock crab

Green sea turtle

Herring

Coral reef

STORIES FROM
Our Coastal Seas

KELP FOREST GUARDIANS

It's springtime off the coast of California, USA. Beneath the surface of this protected marine area lies a magnificent underwater forest of giant kelp. The strands of this seaweed grow up to 50 metres tall. Like a rainforest, the dense canopy provides food and shelter for a lively community.

A sea otter weaves through the kelp fronds, diving for sea urchins. His thick fur keeps him warm in the chilly water.

An urchin looks like a rather prickly meal, but this otter knows that if he can break the shell there's a feast inside. Sea otters are important to the health of the kelp forest because they eat so many sea urchins, which graze on kelp, munching through the tough stems. So, by keeping the urchin numbers down, otters help to protect the precious kelp forests.

The sea otters have a helper in their fight against the spiny grazers: the sheepshead wrasse. This is a fish with powerful teeth that can make short work of the smaller urchins. In the protected area, the otters and wrasse keep the sea urchins under control. Outside the protected area, where otters and wrasse are less active, the urchins have spread across the sea floor. The kelp forests have often disappeared — along with the many species that depend on them.

Sea otter, kelp, sheepshead wrasse and sea urchins

Our Coastal Seas

Coastal recovery

The creation of marine protected areas in coastal waters means wildlife thrives. It's helped otters control the urchin population in the Pacific kelp forests off California, and can even boost the economy in some parts of the world. After years of unregulated fishing around the Medes Islands off the coast of Spain, a square kilometre was made into a protected area. Marine life quickly recovered, and now attracts a carefully controlled tourist industry.

Sheepshead wrasse

SQUADRONS OF THE SEA

From the shores of the Pacific coast off South America, guanay cormorants take wing and head out to sea. The colonies are so vast it takes over an hour for all the cormorants to leave the shore. Inca terns join them, along with pelicans and Peruvian boobies, while sea lions take to the water in huge numbers. By air and sea, this great army of hunters is searching for the same thing: anchovies.

These little fish support the greatest fishery on our planet. Incredibly, this area of the Pacific accounts for a tenth of all the fish we harvest from our oceans every year.

Sea lions are the first to find the schools. As they drive the anchovies to the surface, the pelicans and cormorants plunge in. The boobies strike from heights of 20 metres, hitting the water at 100 kilometres an hour. It's an epic spectacle, with the lives of five million seabirds depending on the great schools, but it used to support five times this number.

Fifty years ago, these colonies all but disappeared because we overfished the waters. Controls were introduced and now fish stocks are recovering, along with the seabirds that depend on them. This demonstrates the astonishing riches our coastal seas can support if we do the right thing to safeguard their future.

Anchovies attacked by sea lions and seabirds

FANCY FISHING

Bottlenose dolphins hunt for fish in the waters of the Florida Everglades using echolocation. They make clicking sounds and use the echoes to work out where their prey can be found. Once the dolphins target their prey, they have their own special way of catching it. A few of them herd the shoal into just the right place, then one dolphin stirs up a ring of mud that surrounds it. In a panic, the fish leap out of the ring . . . and into the jaws of the waiting dolphins.

NIGHT HUNTERS

In the Pacific Ocean off the coast of French Polynesia, grey reef sharks prefer to hunt at night. In darkness, their acute senses give them an advantage over their prey. By day, they like to hang in the current and allow small fish called wrasse to pick at their razor-sharp teeth to keep them nice and clean.

CORAL RICHES

The coral reefs that are commonly found in our warmer shallow coastal waters can be richer in species than tropical rainforests. In Indonesia's Raja Ampat archipelago, a range of reef fish, such as map puffers, glassfish and groupers, can be found amid the colourful coral structures, algae and sponges. But climate change is killing coral reefs. When sea temperatures rise by just a degree or two, corals turn white and die; which is devastating for the wildlife that depends upon them.

JELLYFISH INVASION

Jellyfish are taking over waters once dominated by fish. This can have far-reaching impacts on the food web and ecosystem as a whole. Jellyfish are fascinating creatures so why does this matter? One problem is that they provide very little nourishment compared to energy-rich fish, either to other wildlife or to us. A turtle, seal, seabird or large fish needs to eat far more jellyfish to get as much energy as it would from fish, which means it's much harder work for it to get enough food.

Our Coastal Seas

PROTECTING
Our Coastal Seas

Climate change is having a **BIG IMPACT** on marine life. Burning fossil fuels means water temperatures are rising and the sea is becoming more acidic. This can affect everything from coral reefs to fish stocks.

CLEAN ENERGY can help to save our seas. Cutting down or halting our use of fossil fuels would **SLOW** climate change and help protect every ecosystem in the waters around our shores.

Make more **MARINE PROTECTION ZONES.** Wherever coastal seas are properly protected, which includes controls on what can be fished, marine life **BOUNCES BACK.**

EAT SUSTAINABLE FISH. Look for a trusted certification label when choosing fish. This will help to prevent **OVERFISHING** and lead to lasting stocks in our coastal seas.

Our Deserts & Grasslands

These natural spaces are vast and might often seem empty, but both habitats are vital for wildlife and play an important role in the health of our planet.

Bison graze the grasslands of Badlands National Park, South Dakota

Special Quality

Space is central to grasslands and the life they support. This is where big animals roam, graze and hunt, often in huge numbers, and so their sheer size is important in keeping them healthy. A large space allows herds to move on to fresh grazing, and allows grass to regrow.

Wild meadows

Grassland is not all about the big hunters. Grassy meadows support an extraordinary variety of insects, with different ants, beetles, butterflies and more living in close relationships with each other and with the grasses and flowers.

ALL ABOUT
Our Deserts & Grasslands

In different ways, both deserts and grasslands are essential to the health of our planet. Currently, a fifth of the land on our planet is desert. In this harsh and challenging landscape where rainfall is extremely low, animals have adapted to survive, from beetles and snakes to camels and lizards, as well as plants that need very little water for long periods at a time.

Grasslands cover more than a quarter of the Earth's land. It rains in these regions, but not enough for forests to grow. Grasslands can also be known as meadows, steppes, prairies or savannah.

Around the world, grasslands support spectacular numbers of grazing animals, such as caribou, antelope and zebra. Many of these follow the rains that help grass to grow, and can travel over long distances. These grazing animals stimulate new growth with their trampling feet. They support insect life and wild flowers, keep trees and shrubs from taking over, and provide food for predators.

Grasslands in ecological balance provide enough space for predator and prey to thrive. When that balance comes under threat, through drought or where we have taken over the land to grow food, the ecosystem suffers. In some cases, grasslands become barren and turn into desert. We simply cannot afford to lose more grassland in this way.

Our Deserts & Grasslands

Desert elephant family

STORIES FROM
Our Deserts & Grasslands
A HELPING TRUNK

Fewer than 150 desert elephants remain in Namibia. In this hot, dry and dusty landscape, we find an elderly female leading her herd in a search for food. She knows that the green, leafy ana trees in the distance are a sign of water, and a source of food for the elephants. Her mother first showed her this spot a long time ago. Now, she's teaching her family how to get there.

But today, she encounters a problem. At this time of year, seedpods usually litter the ground under the trees, providing rich food for the elephants. This year, however, the crop has failed. The old elephant has led her herd here for nothing.

The tree canopies are too high for them to even reach and pick off the leaves with their trunks. The family has no option but to move on.

Fortunately, help arrives in time. A bull elephant, standing almost four metres tall, can reach higher and is able to haul down the branches so the group can eat. The old female has known him all her life, and elephants only survive here because of knowledge passed down through generations. With so few desert elephants remaining, and food sources becoming scarce, such knowledge could soon be lost, and elephants may no longer be able to live here.

Our Deserts & Grasslands

Elephant reaching for ana leaves

Cheetahs hunting wildebeest

LIFE ON THE PLAINS

A herd of over one million wildebeest roams the Serengeti in East Africa. They follow the rain as it falls across the plains in order to graze on the newly sprung grass. These vast herds also attract predators, which is a natural part of life here. Cheetahs help keep the wildebeest population from growing too big for the grasslands to sustain.

Right now, a group of five cheetahs are stalking their prey. Four prowl towards the herd, while the fifth uses the long grass to creep around the side unnoticed.

A single cheetah is not strong enough to bring down a wildebeest alone, so it's vital that they work together to be successful. Such dramas are only still possible on the Serengeti because it has been protected for over sixty-five years.

Get smart

If we grow and eat more plant-based foods and eat less meat and dairy — which take up a lot of land to produce — we can feed the planet using fewer resources. We can embrace technology, implementing farming methods that use minimal space, water and pesticides.

BACK FROM THE BRINK

Although species may be suffering where grasslands are under threat, there is still hope. In Mongolia, the once-endangered Przewalski's horses are thriving. Fifty years ago, they were extinct in the wild, but a few adults survived in captivity. Careful breeding from just twelve of these captive animals increased their numbers until there were enough to release on plains largely untouched by humans. Now, numbers top 300, and their future looks more secure.

HEADS UP

Beetles in the roasting Namib have also adapted to survive. When fog rolls off the Atlantic across the desert, they scurry to the top of dunes and stand upside down so that the moisture runs down their bodies and into their mouths.

HOT HEADS

The gemsbok antelopes that roam Africa's Namib desert can survive temperatures of up to 45°C. They are able to conserve water for long periods, while tiny blood vessels in the nose help to cool the blood going into the brain.

FORMER GLORIES

The Great American Plains were once home to millions of bison. This was the true Wild West, until the bison were hunted close to extinction. Today, less than 30,000 remain, with 90 per cent of the prairies now used for agriculture. Over the last century, wild grasslands have lost out to farmland.

It means many of those grazing animals and predators that rely on wild open spaces are being squeezed and even fenced in, but all that may be about to change. These giants are recovering in ranches, tribal lands and national parks, and bison are beginning to roam once more.

PROTECTING
Our Deserts & Grasslands

Grasslands are all about **SPACE**. **IF HERDS CAN'T ROAM,** then land becomes overgrazed, which affects all wildlife.

Overgrazing can lead to some **GRASSLANDS** becoming **DESERTS**. While deserts are precious for some wildlife, we can't afford to **LOSE MORE GRASSLANDS**.

Let's **GET SMART** about farming and grasslands. We can use new technology to farm in **HARMONY WITH NATURE**, and grow crops in clever ways with less impact on the land.

PLANTS NEED LESS SPACE to grow than livestock raised for meat. Eating more **PLANT-BASED FOOD** means we use less grassland for farming.

Our High Seas

Welcome to a world that's a long way from land. Our high seas stretch far and wide. Beyond the boundaries of any country, these wild kingdoms are home to incredible marine life.

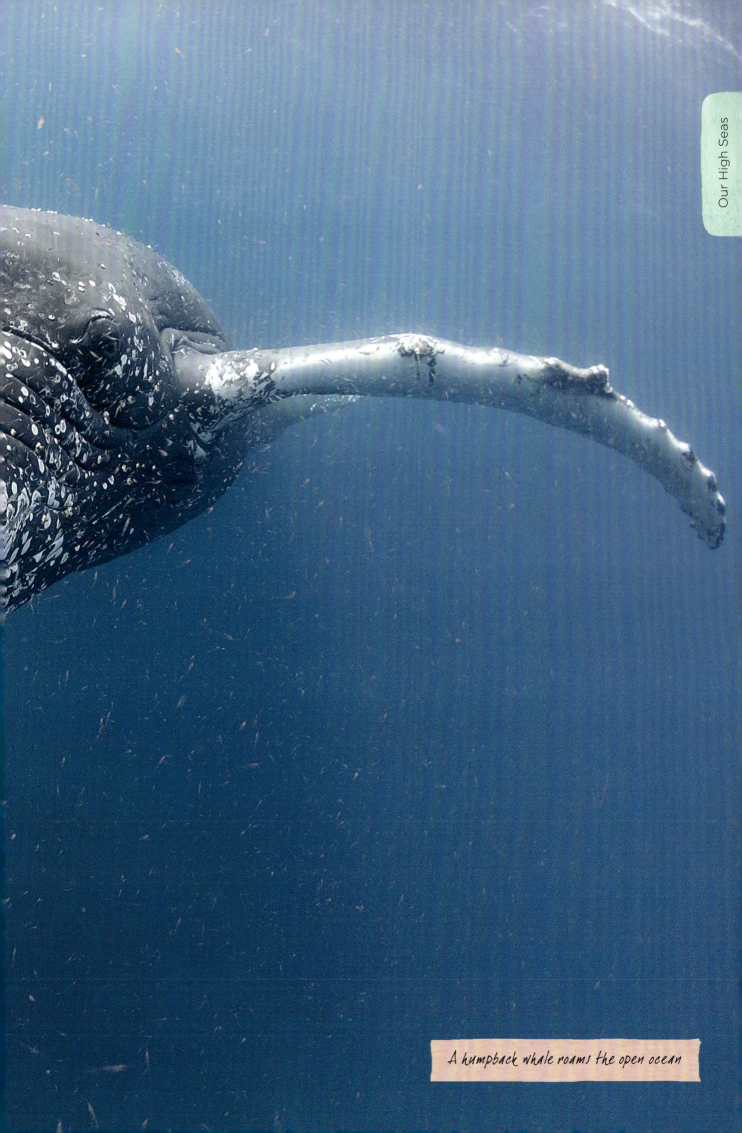

Our High Seas

A humpback whale roams the open ocean

Special Quality
Across the high seas, whales and fish mix up essential nutrients as they migrate through the waters. Hunting in fertile **hotspots**, their poo adds to these nutrients, which allows marine life to thrive.

Spinner dolphins

ALL ABOUT
Our High Seas

Far beyond the shallow coastal waters, the high seas cover nearly half our planet. They are owned by nobody, and are vital to the health of our world.

The high seas support life from the deepest ocean floor to the surface, and even beyond — seabirds soar above and dive into the water after food. The Wilson's petrel is one of the most common — a plucky little bird that flutters above the water and scoops out plankton with its feet.

Sharks patrol the waters, along with fast-moving schools of tuna and squadrons of spinner dolphin up to 1,000 strong. In crossing these watery wildernesses, the spinner often leaps from the water to earn its name by twisting through the air.

In places, the high seas can be more than 11 kilometres deep. Here can be found deep-water giants, such as the 17-metre-long oarfish, and squid the length of buses, along with little lanternfish that can produce their own light. On the ocean bed, far from the surface, cold-coral ecosystems and hydrothermal vents make some parts of the landscape look like an alien world. From top to bottom, the high seas are one of the world's richest spaces for life on the planet. They also face great threats. We once thought that the high seas were too big for us to damage. Now we know this majestic habitat is in danger like never before.

Wandering albatross

Wilson's petrel

Tiger shark

Bluefin tuna

Lanternfish

STORIES FROM
Our High Seas
BIG BLUE

The blue whale is the largest animal ever to have existed on Earth. It weighs up to 200 tonnes and can grow 30 metres long. These graceful giants roam every ocean from the tropics to the icy poles, and yet much of their lives remains a mystery to us. Despite its vast size, the blue whale stays out of sight for much of the time. In fact, we still don't know where they go to breed.

We have only recently discovered a few special places where blue whales come close to shore, like the Gulf of California on Mexico's Pacific coast. Here, we find the world's biggest newborn . . . a baby blue. Just a month old, she's already eight metres long and weighs six tonnes. The mother shelters her young one with a protective fin. They swim side by side, building a close bond before it's time for them to part. Growing up to three tonnes a month, the young blue will eventually leave these sheltered waters for life in the high seas.

Once there were more than 300,000 blue whales worldwide, but in the last century they were hunted so much that only a few thousand survived. Blue whales are now protected, as are other whale species, such as the humpback and minke, and numbers are slowly increasing. Even so, threats remain as we are harming the oceans that are their home.

Blue whale diving

Global cooperation can work

Whales were on the brink of extinction forty years ago but were saved by an international agreement that prevented whaling. Only with global cooperation will our oceans recover, so now it's time to save whole oceans as well as the whales.

Our High Seas

Blue whale mother and baby

HIGH-SEAS HEROES

Most marine activity across the high seas can be found close to the surface. This is because the sun's light and energy can penetrate and fuel the growth of tiny drifting plants called phytoplankton. This is a vital food source for many sea creatures and the basis of the whole ocean food chain. Phytoplankton might be microscopic, but often grow in enormous groups called blooms. These blooms contain millions of individual phytoplankton and can be seen from space. What's more, phytoplankton absorb carbon dioxide from the air and produce almost the same amount of oxygen as the planet's forests and grasslands.

WHALE WHISK

Left undisturbed in the water, phytoplankton will eventually sink down into the depths and decay. This is where whales come in. Take the blue whale, which is as big as a commercial aeroplane. It produces a lot of poo, and this provides marine manure for phytoplankton. What's more, by flicking their tails as they swim and feed, these huge creatures stir up the water and help keep the phytoplankton where it needs to be — near the surface.

Our High Seas

SHINE ON

In the depths of the high seas, far from the reach of sunlight, many species are bioluminescent. This means they create their own natural light to attract prey or to see and avoid predators.

DEEP-SEA TREASURE

We used to think that corals were only found in the warm sunny shallows. Astonishingly, deep-sea corals are thought to cover a greater area of the sea floor, in the cold and dark depths of the high seas, than their shallow-water relatives.

PROTECTING
Our High Seas

HOPE for the **HIGH SEAS!**
Recycling responsibly is one thing, but imagine a world in which nothing is thrown away. If we seek out products designed to last, or that can be upgraded and repaired but never wasted, then our magnificent oceans will **THRIVE.**

SAVE OUR PHYTOPLANKTON.
To protect these microscopic but mighty marine plants, we need to **CARE** for the marine life that relies upon them, from the smallest fish to the largest whale.

RETHINK high-seas fishing.
It's challenging and expensive, and many high-seas species are endangered, but if we choose only fish from **SUSTAINABLE** coastal waters, high-seas stocks will return. That's good for the phytoplankton and **GREAT** for our planet.

Put a **STOP** to the **PLASTIC PERIL.**
When discarded plastic breaks down into fragments in sea water, it can get inside plankton. As a result, this **WASTE** is slowly contaminating the marine food chain. We have to **CHANGE OUR WAYS.**

Our Fresh Water

Without fresh water, life on Earth wouldn't exist. Every animal and plant that lives on land depends upon it — including humans. Fresh water is the most precious resource on our planet, but we must allow it to flow freely.

Pelicans on Lake Brewster, Australia

Our Fresh Water

ALL ABOUT
Our Fresh Water

Despite its life-giving importance, fresh water adds up to less than three per cent of the total water on Earth. The rest is salt water in the seas and oceans. What's more, almost all our fresh water is locked up in ice caps or glaciers, although some of this is released as meltwater when the ice retreats every spring. Even more fresh water is buried deep underground. In fact, at any one time, only a tiny fraction of the total water on Earth runs through rivers and streams, ponds, lakes and wetlands. Even so, it's this flow of fresh water that's essential to the health of the freshwater environment and everything that relies upon it.

Fresh water is the key to life on our planet and essential to human beings. We drink it to stay alive, and use it to stay clean and to water our crops. We also use it to produce electricity through hydropower and for cooling in thermal power stations.

Nature relies on fresh water too. Freshwater habitats are home to more than ten per cent of all the world's known animals, from dragonflies and kingfishers to ospreys and bears. Almost half of all known fish species exist in fresh waterways. Some, such as salmon and catfish, rely on the flow of fresh water to travel vast distances to complete their life cycles. Fresh water also helps to control the temperature of the land and sea, and even acts like a huge conveyor belt, transporting nutrients that make soil fertile.

Black bears, bald eagles and thousands of salmon thrive in this freshwater habitat

Our Fresh Water

Special Quality

In fresh waters, it's all about **flow**. The free movement of water in rivers, streams and wetlands is vital for wildlife when it comes to feeding, breeding and migration.

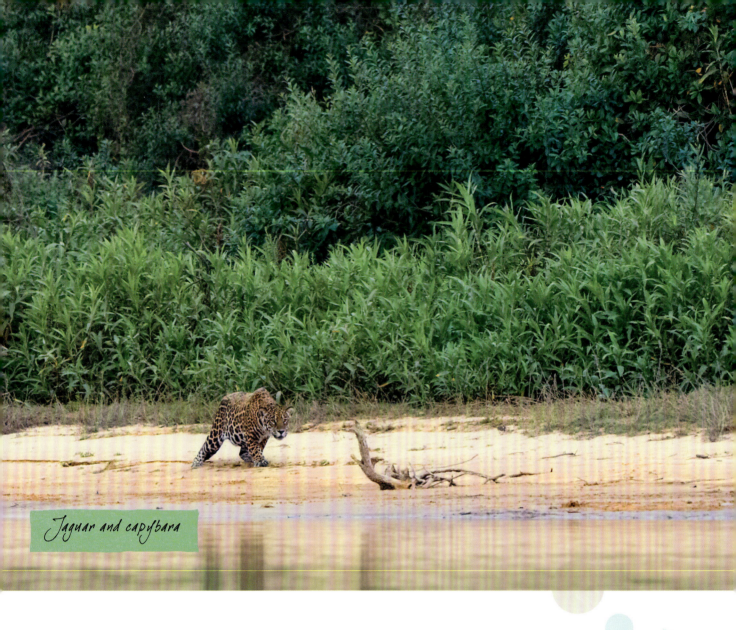

Jaguar and capybara

STORIES FROM
Our Fresh Water
ROAMING THE RIVERBANK

When rain falls over the plains of Brazil, it creates the largest tropical wetland on Earth — the Pantanal — and draws all manner of animals to the riverbanks.

A jaguar prowls towards a pair of capybara standing in the shallows. Capybara are the largest living rodents in the world. The jaguar may be a top predator, but the capybara are more nimble once they flee into the water, and this time the chance of a meal is lost. The jaguar slinks on.

Perhaps it's time to try a different prey. The caiman is like an alligator, but with longer teeth.

It's basking in the shallows below the bank, unaware of the approaching jaguar. Tackling one of these would be risky, but this jaguar has a technique.

Splash! The jaguar takes the caiman by surprise by leaping from above. Immediately the caiman rolls to try to drown it. Predator and prey seem evenly matched, but the jaguar hangs on until finally he wins the battle . . .

Moments like these take place across the wetlands of the Pantanal. This is nature as it should be. Whatever the story, water is at the heart of it.

Our Fresh Water

Jaguar and caiman

DROUGHT DRAMA

In some parts of Tanzania, East Africa, the water flow from many rivers has been diverted for farming. This means that during droughts the great waterways shrink to isolated pools, and this affects the wildlife.

Hippopotamuses depend on free-flowing water to keep cool during the day. Now, they're forced to wallow in mud. As the water level falls still further, the hippos find themselves crammed together. That's when tempers begin to fray.

Buffaloes are forced to the same small drinking spots as the lions that prey upon them. As the drought continues the buffaloes begin to weaken, and the odds change in the lions' favour.

The hardships of the dry season have always been part of life on East Africa's plains. But as the planet warms and we take so much water for our own needs, the droughts are becoming more frequent and severe.

Hippopotamuses

Super-users
Humans use over ten billion tonnes of fresh water daily – we transport water from wherever it should be to wherever we want it. We've turned torrents into trickles and the repercussions are devastating... Rivers dry out, fish stocks plummet, crops fail, and drinking water disappears.

MAYFLY MAYHEM

Female mayflies can't waste time after mating. At dusk on the tributaries of Europe's River Danube, female mayflies swarm into the air. Then the race is on to fly upstream and lay their eggs before they die from exhaustion just a few hours later.

PADDLE POWER

The rivers of the Andes in South America run fast and strong. For those that can cope with the currents and the chilly waters, there is food — mainly insects and their larvae — to be plucked from just below the surface. Torrent ducks, strong swimmers and plucky divers able to pick what little food there is from the riverbed, are designed for the job.

SHELL SHOW

Competition among the cichlid fish is intense in the crowded waters of Africa's Lake Tanganyika. To attract the attention of a female, a male callipterus cichlid collects shells. He isn't just trying to impress her, however. The female cichlid is so tiny she can slip inside a shell to lay her eggs. Once the eggs are fertilised by the male, she will guard them for up to a fortnight before they hatch.

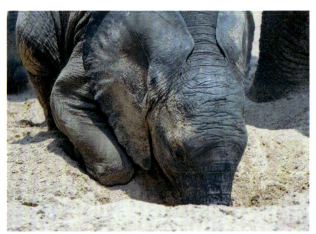

DROUGHT DIGGERS

In Tanzania, in the same drought-hit drinking spots used by hippos and buffaloes, elephants reach their river and find it has run dry. They use their trunks to dig holes where the water once flowed. Their extraordinary sense of smell helps them to locate where water lies closest to the surface. In severe droughts, the wells they dig can be their lifeline.

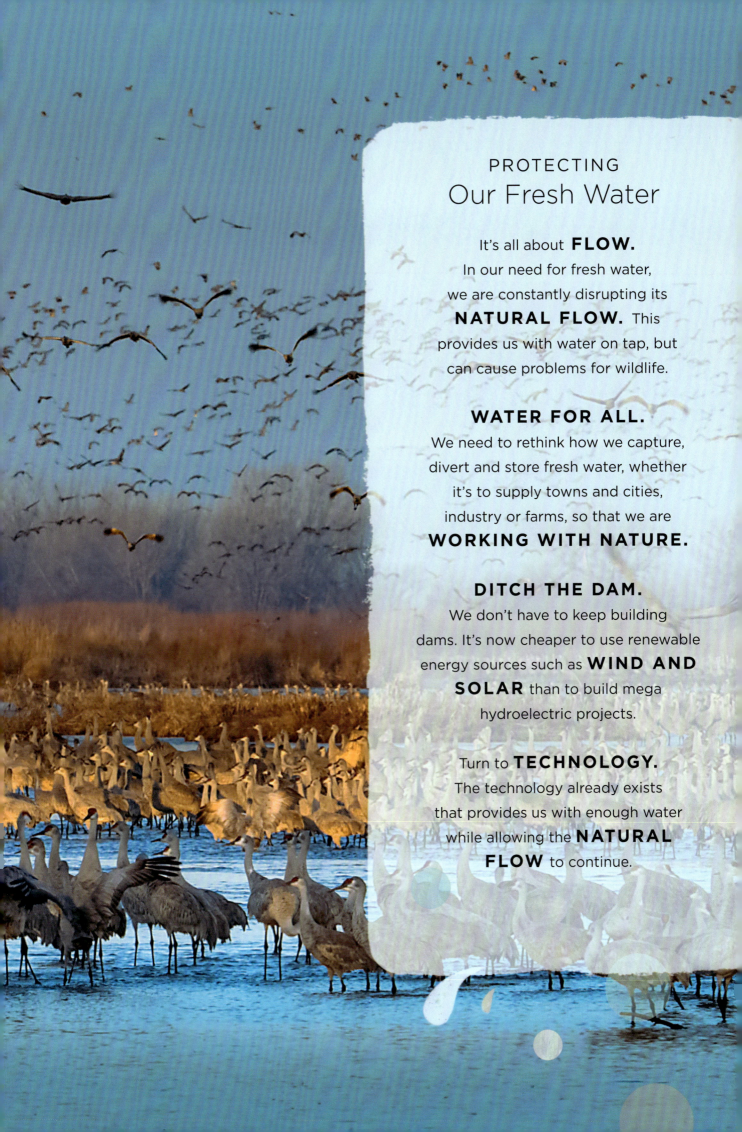

PROTECTING
Our Fresh Water

It's all about **FLOW.**
In our need for fresh water, we are constantly disrupting its **NATURAL FLOW.** This provides us with water on tap, but can cause problems for wildlife.

WATER FOR ALL.
We need to rethink how we capture, divert and store fresh water, whether it's to supply towns and cities, industry or farms, so that we are **WORKING WITH NATURE.**

DITCH THE DAM.
We don't have to keep building dams. It's now cheaper to use renewable energy sources such as **WIND AND SOLAR** than to build mega hydroelectric projects.

Turn to **TECHNOLOGY.**
The technology already exists that provides us with enough water while allowing the **NATURAL FLOW** to continue.

Our Forests

Without forests, life as we know it wouldn't exist. They are key to our climate and, together with jungles, they are home to half the planet's land-living species, and yet we continue to cut them down. The great thing about forests is that they can bounce back, but we must give them a chance.

Great hornbills battle in the canopy of India's Western Ghats forest

Our Forests

Special Quality

Resilience is key to seasonal forests. When left to adapt over time, with a mix of old and new trees, forests can spring back to life, even after a fire.

Fox in a Ukrainian forest

ALL ABOUT
Our Forests

Forests and jungles cover almost a third of all the Earth's land area (see pages 24—33 for more on jungles). There are different kinds of forest. Each contains a delicate balance of trees and other plants, animals, fungi and bacteria.

Some forests are in temperate parts of the world, where there are four seasons each year, with wide changes in temperature and daylight hours. Many seasonal forest trees are deciduous, which means they shed their leaves in winter to avoid damage by cold and snow. Other seasonal forests consist of mainly conifer trees. Conifers have needle-shaped leaves with a waxy coating that helps them cope with extremely cold or dry conditions. They keep their leaves all year round.

The largest seasonal forest on Earth is called the boreal. It's spread across continents just south of the Arctic, from North America to Russia and Europe's Scandinavian regions. With long, cold winters and short summers, the boreal forest contains over 750 billion trees. Not only does this store vast amounts of the world's carbon, the boreal forest is home to a range of animals, such as elk, bison, moose, beavers and bears, birds including cranes and warblers, and insect species from aphids to beetles and sawflies.

Forest regions close to the equator are tropical, with a steady warm and wet climate. These are tropical rainforests, sometimes known as jungles, and have particularly thick vegetation and a wide variety of species. In the Indian Ocean, the island of Madagascar is home to a unique tropical forest teeming with life. Cut off from the rest of the world for millions of years, the Madagascan animals and plants have evolved into forms quite different from anywhere else. Here, you'll find creatures with weird and wonderful names like the panther chameleon and tomato frog, as well as the cat-like fossa.

Baobab leaf

Oak leaf

Common beech leaf

Loblolly pine leaves

Redwood leaves

Rubber tree leaves

Silver fir leaves

Broadleaf maple leaf

STORIES FROM
Our Forests
ON THE PROWL

The Siberian tiger is able to patrol a territory of almost 2,000 square kilometres. This species is under threat, with fewer than 600 in the wild worldwide. It is mainly found in the boreal forests of the Russian Far East and areas of China. In areas where prey is in short supply, this rare but magnificent creature needs a vast hunting ground to keep itself alive during the long winter.

The Siberian tiger preys on rabbits and hares, as well as larger animals such as deer, moose and even bears. It's a clever beast, and tracks wild boar through the forest. The wild boar is keeping its eye out for pine cones, which make a tasty treat. Where there are pine cones there are likely to be boar, but will one emerge from the undergrowth? As the boar knows the tiger might be watching, this game of hide-and-seek can go on for a long time across huge areas of forest. When food is in short supply, the tiger can only hope that the boar will risk its life for a chance to eat.

Siberian tiger stalking wild boar

Our Forests

Siberian tiger

Ring-tailed lemur

WILD AND WEIRD

Welcome to the remote island of Madagascar — a tropical forest home to wildlife found nowhere else on Earth.

The lemur is one of the many strange creatures to be found in the island's forest community. There are more than a hundred species and subspecies of lemur that are unique to Madagascar, including the ring-tailed lemur. This sociable little creature lives in groups of up to thirty animals, and is vital to the survival of some tree species on the island. This is because the tree fruits form a central part of the lemur's diet, and the seeds are spread in their droppings.

Like so many creatures of Madagascar, this lemur is an endangered species. The fact is most of the island's forests have been lost to farming or cut down for timber, and the wildlife is under threat. It's possible to protect this unique environment through careful forest management, but time is running out.

FOREST GIANTS

The last of the great redwood forests are found in North America. Not so long ago, these gigantic conifers grew throughout the Pacific Northwest. Now less than five per cent remain, and are able to grow all year round because of the warm air from the Pacific.

CONE CARRIERS

There are more than 115 species of pine trees, forty of which are most common. These conifer trees produce bundles of waxy needles rather than leaves, along with cones that contain pollen or seeds.

WATER WONDERS

Found in India, Africa, Australia and Madagascar, the baobab can contain thousands of litres of water inside its trunk. This makes it a vital resource for local wildlife in dry conditions, and is the reason why it's also sometimes known as the 'bottle tree'.

Redwood tree

Pine tree — *Baobab tree*

Our Forests

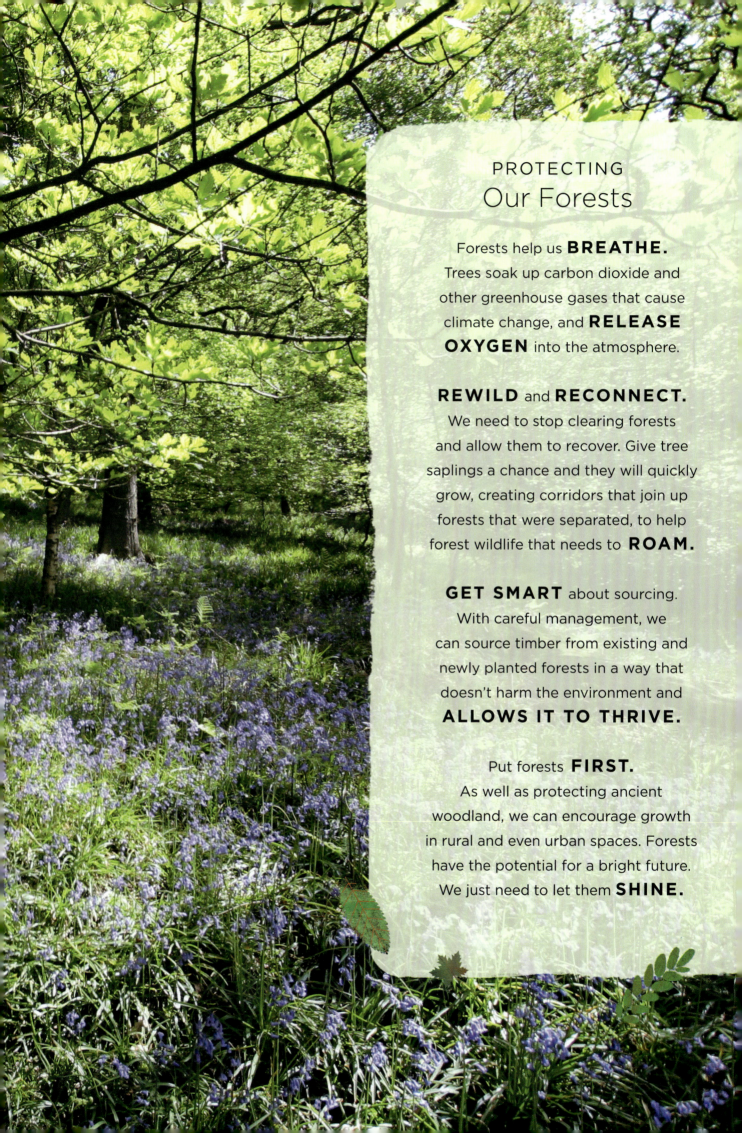

PROTECTING
Our Forests

Forests help us **BREATHE.** Trees soak up carbon dioxide and other greenhouse gases that cause climate change, and **RELEASE OXYGEN** into the atmosphere.

REWILD and **RECONNECT.** We need to stop clearing forests and allow them to recover. Give tree saplings a chance and they will quickly grow, creating corridors that join up forests that were separated, to help forest wildlife that needs to **ROAM.**

GET SMART about sourcing. With careful management, we can source timber from existing and newly planted forests in a way that doesn't harm the environment and **ALLOWS IT TO THRIVE.**

Put forests **FIRST.** As well as protecting ancient woodland, we can encourage growth in rural and even urban spaces. Forests have the potential for a bright future. We just need to let them **SHINE.**

One Chance

Our planet is our home. It provides us with food, water and shelter, and has allowed us to grow as a species for over 200,000 years. Now we have arrived at a moment where we must rethink our relationship with the Earth. Why? Because we have changed it so much that for the first time in our planet's history, the global connections that all living things rely on are breaking.

Each of the seven biomes we have explored is nature's response to a particular climate and geography. They have all evolved special qualities that support life there, from jungle diversity to the space that is key to our grasslands, to the resilience of forests and the flow of fresh water. Then there's the importance of polar ice, the fertile hotspots in our high seas where whales and big fish stir up microscopic nutrients to support the marine food chain, and the abundance of fish in our coastal waters. Through our actions, however, all this is under threat . . .

We must recognise that each biome plays an essential role in the health of the ultimate ecosystem — Planet Earth itself. If our world is to remain healthy, stable and productive, then all the biomes must function properly. Harming just one habitat has global consequences and affects us all.

If we are to take responsibility for our actions, we must begin by recognising that every breath we take and all the food we eat comes from the natural world. We are one ecosystem. It is central to human life, and we are in danger of wrecking it.

Over time, we have turned from a species that lived in harmony with nature to one that has taken advantage of it. Nature cannot support our needs if we continue in this way. We need to restore the balance.

One Future

We urgently need to find ways to do something radical — to live sustainably. But just how do we create a future in which both people and nature are in harmony? This is the biggest question of our times.

The good news is that human beings are able to work together and solve problems. We also have the technology and the resources to change our way of life on a global scale. The challenge is to do so in a way that puts the planet first. We know that nature will recover if we give it a chance. We can rewild the world, but we have to begin right now. How? By making sure that everything we do in life does as little degradation and harm as possible to the environment.

We can phase out fossil fuels and replace them with renewable sources of energy. This will slow the warming of the planet — which is causing the polar ice to shrink — and provide clean air for us all.

We can reduce our consumption of meat in the western world, and eat only meat and fish from the most sustainable sources. By having a more plant-based diet and using the latest technology in farming, we'll require less space and resources to feed ourselves. This will save grasslands, jungles and forests, and cut down on our demand for fresh water.

We can work together to manage our oceans and create a global network of no-fishing zones. This would allow fish stocks to recover and provide more fish for us to eat.

These are big changes, but we all have a role to play in making them happen. By transforming attitudes, raising awareness and pushing to improve our relationship with the world at every level, we can become a species in balance with nature once again.

Then we can take pride in our planet — the only home we have.

Our Amazing Planet
FILMING BEHIND THE SCENES OF THE SERIES

Glossary

algae a group of plant-like living things that usually live in water. They absorb sunlight and carbon dioxide and give off oxygen. Many types of algae are microscopic, but seaweeds are also algae.

archipelago a group of islands.

atmosphere a thick layer of air that surrounds the Earth.

bacteria a large group of microscopic living things. Some cause disease, but many are very important for digestion, helping things to rot and keeping nature in balance.

barren a landscape that is dry and bare where not many plants or animals can live.

bioluminescent the ability of a living thing to produce light.

biome *see* habitat

canopy the layer of tree branches and leaves that spreads out at the top of a jungle or forest.

carbon dioxide a gas that is found in air. The amount of carbon dioxide in the air is increasing, which is causing global warming and climate change.

carnivore an animal that eats other animals.

climate change variation in the Earth's climate over a period of time. The overall average temperature of the Earth is now rising (this is sometimes called global warming), which is affecting climate. Human actions, such as burning fossil fuels and cutting down forests, are making this happen.

colony a large group of the same type of animal living together.

degradation damage to land making it worn out or poor, for example by deforestation or the wrong kind of farming.

diversity lots of different kinds of animals and plants living in a particular place.

echolocation finding the way or finding prey by making sounds and then using the echoes to tell where things are.

ecosystem a particular place where different plants and animals live together, and the relationship between all those plants and animals and the place where they live. An ecosystem can be a small corner of a jungle or an individual lake, or a great forest, or the whole Earth.

endangered at high risk of dying out altogether.

evaporation when water, for example the moisture on rain-soaked leaves, changes into water vapour and rises into the air.

evolved developed and changed slowly over long periods of time.

extinction dying out altogether. If an animal or plant is extinct, there are no more of them alive anywhere in the world.

fertile able to support healthy living things. A fertile place is one where many plants and animals can live and thrive. Fertile also means able to produce young.

fertilised when an egg is fertilised, a baby can start growing inside it. When soil is fertilised, this means nutrients that help plants grow have been added to it.

food chain a group of living things that are connected because each one eats another one in the chain. Plants and algae are at the bottom of food chains. Animals eat the plants, and in turn other animals eat the plant-eaters. At the top of the food chain are the top predators — nothing eats them.

fossil fuels substances such as oil, natural gas and coal that were made millions of years ago from the remains of prehistoric living things. Burning fossil fuels provides energy but releases pollution into the air. It also releases carbon dioxide, a greenhouse gas, which is helping to cause global warming.

glacier a body of slowly moving thick ice that covers a large area of land. Glaciers stay frozen all year round, although some melting happens each summer. Glaciers are added to by fresh snow and refreezing in winter.

graze to eat grass or other plants where they grow.

habitat a place where particular animals and plants naturally live.

hotspot a place where there is a particularly high number of different living things.

hydropower power generated from moving water.

hydrothermal vent a hole in the ocean floor where hot water, heated deep within the Earth's crust, gushes out. Lots of nutrients are found in these water spurts, and many strange creatures live around such holes.

lagoon an area of calm seawater cut off from the open sea, for instance by a coral reef.

marine to do with the sea.

microscopic something so small that it can only be seen using a microscope.

migrating moving every year from one part of the world to another, usually to reach a good place to breed or find food.

nutrients substances that animals and plants need to help them grow and stay healthy.

oxygen a gas that is found in the air. Plants give off oxygen, and animals breathe it in.

renewable energy is energy generated by natural resources that constantly renew, like sunshine, geothermal heat, wind, rain, tides and waves. We use technology or engineering to collect it, and the best thing about it is that it will never run out.

rodent a mammal belonging to a group that includes mice, rats, squirrels, agouti and capybaras. They all have very sharp front teeth.

species a particular group of living things that share characteristics and can breed with each other. There are millions of different species on our planet.

sustainable using natural resources in such a way that they are not used up, protecting and helping living resources to survive and be healthy in the future.

territory an area of land that an animal regards as its own and defends against others.

whaling hunting and killing whales.

wilderness an area of land or sea that is wild and not used by people.

Index

A
Africa
  fresh water 70, 71
  grasslands 50, *52*, 70
  jungles 27
agoutis 27
agriculture *see also* farming
albatrosses *21*, 57
algae 16, 41, 88
Amazon jungle 26, 27, 30
anchovies *40*
Antarctica 16, 21
antelope 8, 47, 51
ants
  carpenter 30
  leafcutter 27
apes
  gorillas *24-25*, 27
  orangutans 8, *28-29*
Arctic 16
  animals 20, 21
atmosphere 16, 33, 83, 88

B
babies
  albatross 21
  gorilla *24-25*
  orangutan 8, *28-29*
  penguin 18
  polar bear 16, *20*
  whale, blue 58-59, *59*
bacteria 77, 88
baobab trees *77*, 81
bears *66*, 77, 78
beetles 46-47, 51, *77*
bioluminescence 61, 88
biomes *10-11*, 84
birds
  albatrosses *21*, 57
  birds of paradise *31*
  boobies, Peruvian 40
  cormorants, guanay 40
  ducks, torrent 71
  eagles, Philippine *31*
  hornbills, great *74-75*
  pelicans 40, *64-65*
  penguins 8, 16, 17, 18, *19*
  petrels, Wilson's 57
birds of paradise 31

bison *12-13*, *44-45*, 51, 77
blooms 60
blubber 18, 21
blue whales *8-9*, 58-59, *59*, 60
boar, wild 78
boobies, Peruvian 40
Borneo 8, 31
Brazil 68
broadleaf maple tree 77
buffaloes 70

C
caimans 69
capybaras 68, *69*, 89
carbon 23, 77
carbon dioxide 16, 33, 60, 83, 88
caribou 47
cats
  cheetahs 8, *50*
  jaguars 68
  leopards, clouded *31*
  lions 70
  tigers, Siberian 78, *79*
cheetahs 8, *50*
climate change 20, 21, 83, 88
coastal seas *10-11*, 12, 34-43
common beech tree 77
Congo 25, 27
conifers 77, 81
coral reefs 37, *41*, 61
cormorants, guanay 40
crabs 37
crustaceans 21

D
Danube, River 71
deforestation 28-29, 80
deserts *10-11*, 47-49, 51
  beetles 51
  elephants 48, *48-49*, 71
  gemsbok antelopes 51
  life 47-49, 51
  Namib desert 51
diversity 27, 84, 88
dolphins
  bottlenose *41*
  spinner 56, *57*
droughts 47, 70, 71
ducks, torrent 71

E
eagles, Philippine *31*
echolocation 41, 88
economy 39
ecosystems 84, 88
  coastal seas 37
  grasslands 47
  jungles 24, 30
elephants 48, *48-49*, 71
endangered species 51, 80
equator 27, 77
extinction 9, 51, 58, 88

F
farming
  and deforestation 28-29, 80
  future of 53, 85
  loss of grasslands 51
  and rivers 70
fish 34, 37, 41
  anchovies 40
  freshwater 66, 71
  lanternfish 57
  oarfish 57
  salmon 8, 66
  sharks, grey reef *36*, 41
  tuna 57
  wrasse 38, *39*, 41
fishing 37, 39, 40, 41, 85
food chain, ocean 16, 21, 37, 60, 84, 88
forests *10-11*, 12, 74-83
  boars 78
  boreal 77, 78
  carbon 23, 77
  lemurs 80
  life 76-81
  location 77
  Madagascar 77, 80, 81
  rainforests 28, 31, 77, 80
  seasons 77
  tigers, Siberian 78, *79*
  see also jungles
fossil fuels 16, 89
foxes *76*
freshwater biome
  10-11, 12, 64-73
frozen worlds *10-11*, 12, 14-23
  albatrosses *21*
  Antarctica 16, 21

90

Arctic 16, 20, 21
elephant seals 18
food chain 21
ice 16-17, 20, 21, 66
krill 16, 20, *21*
leopard seals 18
life 16, 18-21
location 12, 14
melting 16, 20, 21, 66
mountains 16
nutrients 16
penguins 8, 16, 17, 18, *19*, 21
polar bears 8, *14-15*, 16, 17, *20*, *22*, 84
south pole 16
Southern Ocean 16, 21
walruses *21*
whales 20, 21
winter 16, 20
fruits 8, 27, 80
fungi 77
  grown by ants 27
  Ophiocordyceps 30
future, preparing for the 85

G

gemsbok antelopes *51*
glaciers 66, 89
global warming 16, 20, 21, 88, 89
gorillas, western lowland 27
grasslands *10-11*, 12, 44, 46-47, 50-51
  bison *12-13*, *44-45*, 51
  cheetahs 8, *50*
  grazing animals 47
  Great American Plains 51
  horses, Przewalski's 51
  life 47, 50-51
  Mongolia 51
  wildebeest *50*
grazing 47, 89
Great American Plains 51

H

habitat
  see also biomes
herds 50
herring *37*
high seas *10-11*, 12, 54-63

hippopotamuses 70
hornbills, great *74-75*
horses, Przewalski's 51
hotspots 56, 89
humans 9
  deforestation by 28-29, 80
  farming 28-29, 51, 53, 70, 80, 85
  fishing 37, 39, 40, 41, 43, 85
  the future 85
  and melting sea ice 16
  use of fossil fuels 16
  and water 66
humpback whales 20, 21, *54-55*, 58
hunting 8, 20, 21, 31, 41, 50, 78
hydrothermal vents 57, 89

I

ice 16-17, 66, 89
  melting 16, 20, 21, 66
  sea 16, 20
India 81
Indonesia 28, 41
insects 71
  ants 27, 30
  beetles 46-47, *51*, *77*
  mayflies 71

J

jaguars 68
jellyfish *41*
jungles *10-11*, 12, 24-33, 77
  Amazon 26, 30
  Borneo 8, 31
  deforestation 28-29
  diversity 27, 84
  largest 26
  life 26, 27, 28, 30, 31
  location 27
  palm oil 28, 29, 33
  Philippine islands 31
  trees 27, 28, 29

K

kelp 37, 38
killer whales 21
krill 16, 20, *21*

L

lanternfish *57*
leafcutter ants 27
leaves 27, 30, 48, 77
lemurs 80
leopards, clouded *31*
lions 70
loblolly pine tree *77*

M

Madagascar 77, 80, 81
mammals
  agoutis 27
  antelope 8, 47, 51
  bears 66, 77, 78
  bison *12-13*, *44-45*, 51, 77
  boar, wild 78
  buffaloes 70
  cheetahs 8, *50*
  dolphins 41, *56*, 57
  elephants 48, *48-49*, 71
  gemsbok antelopes *51*
  gorillas *24-25*, 27
  hippopotamuses 70
  horses, Przewalski's *51*
  lemurs 80
  leopards, clouded 31
  orangutans 8, *28-29*
  polar bears 8, *14-15*, 16, 17, *20*, *22*, 84
  sea lions 40
  sea otters *38*, 39
  tigers, Siberian 78, *79*
  walruses *21*
  whales 9, 20, 21, 55, 56, 58-59, 60
manta rays 37
mayflies 71
migration 8, 16, 67, 89
Mongolia 51
mountains 16

N

Namib desert 51
Namibia 48
narwhals 16
national parks 51
North America 45, 77, 81

91

Index

USA 38
north pole 23
nutrients 16, 56, 60, 66, 84, 89

O

oak trees 77
oarfish 57
oceans
　Arctic 16
　coasts 34-43
　food chain 16, 21, 37, 60, 84, 88
　high seas 54-63
　Pacific 40, 41
　Southern 16, 21
orangutans 8, *28-29*
orcas 21
otters, sea *38*, 39
oxygen 33, 60, 83, 89

P

Pacific Ocean 40, 41
palm oil 28, 29, 33
Pantanal 68
parenting 8, 18, 20, 21, 28, 37, 58
pelicans 40, *64-65*
penguins 16, 17, 21
　emperor 8
　king *18*, *19*
petrels, Wilson's 57
phytoplankton 21, 60, 63
pine trees 81
plankton 16, 57, 63
plants
　forest 77
　jungle 27
　sea 37, 60
　see also trees
pods 21
polar bears 8, *14-15*, 16, 17, 20, *22*, 84
　hunting 8, 20
poles, the 16-17
predators 20, 21, 31, 37, 47, 50, 68
protected areas 38, 39, 44, 50

R

rain 47, 68
rainforests 77, 80
　see also jungles
Raja Ampat 41
redwood trees 77, 81
renewable energy 85, 89
rivers 66, 68, 69
rodents 68, 89
rubber tree 77

S

salmon 8, 66
sea lions 40
sea otters *38*, 39
sea urchins 38, 39
seabirds 18, 37, 40, 41, 57
seals 20, 21
　elephant 18
　leopard 18
　monk 37
seas
　coastal seas *10-11*, 12, 34-43
　high seas *10-11*, 54-63
　sea ice 16, 20
　sea levels 17
seaweed 38
seeds 27, 48, 80, 81
Serengeti 50
sharks 37, 57
　grey reef *36*
silver fir tree 77
soil 66
South America
　coastal seas 40
　jungles 27
　rivers 71
South Georgia 18
south pole 16, 23
Southern Ocean 16, 21
Spain 39
sponges 37, 41
squid 57
strangler fig 27
Sumatra 28
sunlight 17, 37, 61

T

Tanzania 70, 71
temperature
　and fresh water 66
　rising 16, 20, 23, 43
　see also climate change
tigers, Siberian 78, *79*
tourism 39
trees 76, 77, 80, 81
　ana trees 48, *49*
　baobab *77*, 81
　Brazil-nut 27
　common beech 77
　conifers *77*, 81
　deciduous 77
　deforestation 28-29, 80
　loblolly pine 77
　oak *77*
　pine *77*, 78, 81
　redwoods *77*, 81
　rubber *77*
　silver fir *77*
　strangler figs 27
tuna 57
turtles *34-35*, *37*, 41

U

USA 38

W

walruses *21*
water
　drinking 51, 64, 70
　freshwater biome *10-11*, 64-73
whales 9, 55, 56, 60
　blue *8-9*, 58-59, *59*, 60
　humpback 20, 21, *54-55*, 58
　killer 21
　narwhals 16
whaling 20, 58, 89
wildebeest *50*
wrasse fish 38, *39*, 41

Y

young
　albatross *21*
　orangutan 8, *28-29*
　penguin 18
　polar bear *20*
　whale, blue 58-59, *59*

Z

zebra 47

ACKNOWLEDGEMENTS & PHOTO CREDITS

Colin Butfield Executive Consultant Editor
Colin has been closely involved in Our Planet since its inception, working alongside the series producers and Netflix. His involvement includes acting as the scientific and conservation advisor on the Netflix series and building the story through OurPlanet.com, which not only shows the issues the planet is facing but the solutions. Colin has worked at WWF for nearly fifteen years and has worked on many conservation issues around the world.

Richard Jones Artist
Richard graduated from University of Plymouth with a first class degree in Graphic Design and Illustration. Richard's illustration style is unique, working with stunning layered textures, he creates stand-out illustration which has won him acclaim the world over.

Matt Whyman Author
Matt is a bestselling author who has written widely for all ages.
His books include *Walking With Sausage Dogs* and *The Unexpected Genius of Pigs*.

Silverback Films
With special thanks to Silverback Films, whose award-winning team filmed and produced the *Our Planet* series.

WWF
With special thanks to WWF for supporting *Our Planet* as scientific advisors, helping to showcase some of the most pressing challenges and solutions facing our natural world.

Particular thanks to
Paige Ashton, Catherine Brereton, Adam Chapman, Dan Clamp, Darren Clementson, Claire Cockett, Rebecca Coombs, Huw Cordey, Alastair Fothergill, Ewan Guilder, Kelvin Jones, Sophie Lanfear, Our Planet Team, Laura Meacham, Eve Murchison, Philippa Milnes-Smith, Ed Partridge, Hugh Pearson, Keith Scholey, Mandi Stark, Carrie Watson, Jeff Wilson, Laura Winn and the WWF Science Team.

Paul Stewart/Netflix/Silverback (page 6, tree frog)

Foreword
Cristina Casillas Lopez/Silverback/Netflix (pages 8–9, whale)

One Planet
Jeffrey West (pages 12–13, bison)

One Frozen Worlds
David Reid/Silverback/Netflix (pages 14–15, polar bear)
Sophie Lanfear/Silverback/Netflix (pages 16–17, ice), (page 21, walrus), (page 21, albatross chick), (pages 22–23, broken sea-ice)
Oliver Scholey/Silverback/Netflix (page 19, penguin chicks)
naturepl.com/Visuals Unlimited/WWF (page 21, krill)
Hector Skevington-Postles/Jamie McPherson/Silverback/Netflix (page 21, orca and penguin)

Our Jungles
Ted Giffords/Silverback/Netflix (pages 24–25, gorillas)
Huw Cordey/Silverback/Netflix (page 29, young orangutan), (pages 32–33, jungle)
Richard Kirby/Silverback/Netflix (page 30, zombie ant)

Our Coastal Seas
Oliver Scholey/Silverback/Netflix (pages 34–35, green sea turtle)
Gisle Sverdrup/Silverback/Netflix (page 36, sharks), (page 41, grey reef sharks/compass jellyfish)
Jeff Hester/Silverback/Netflix (page 39, sheepshead wrasse)
Jamie McPherson/Silverback/Netflix (page 41, bottlenose dolphins)
Grace Frank/Silverback/Netflix (page 41, coral reefs)

Jürgen Freund/WWF (pages 42–43, fish by coral reef)

Our Deserts and Grasslands
WWF-US/Clay Bolt (pages 44–45, bison)
Jamie McPherson/Silverback/Netflix (pages 48–49, elephants)
Jamie McPherson/Silverback/Netflix (page 50, cheetah hunting wildebeest), (pages 52–53, elephant)

Our High Seas
Steve Benjamin/Silverback/Netflix (page 54–55, humpback whale)
Howard Bourne/Silverback/Netflix (page 56, spinner dolphins)
Oliver Scholey/Hector Skevington-Postles/Silverback/Netflix (page 59, blue whales)
Pascal Kobeh (pages 62–63, tuna in net)

Our Fresh Water
Mal Carnegie/Silverback/Netflix (pages 64–65, pelicans)
Gavin Thurston/Silverback/Netflix (pages 68–69, Jaguar and capybara)
Ted Giffords/Silverback/Netflix (page 71, mass emergence of mayflies in Hungary)
Angel Fitor/Silverback/Netflix (page 71, a male *Lamprologus callipterus*)
Barrie Britton/Silverback/Netflix (page 71, torrent duck)
Owen Prumm/Silverback/Netflix (page 71, baby elephant)
Sophie Darlington/Silverback/Netflix (pages 72–73, sandhill cranes)

Our Forests
Sandesh Kadur/Silverback/Netflix (pages 74–75, great hornbills)

Kieran O'Donovan/Silverback/Netflix (page 76, fox), (page 79, Siberian tiger)
WWF/Martina Lippuner (page 80, ring-tailed lemur)
Steve Morgan/WWF (pages 82–83, bluebells in bloom, UK)

One Chance, One Future
Jamie McPherson/Silverback/Netflix (pages 84–85, polar bears)

Our Amazing Planet (page 86, clockwise from top)
Oliver Scholey/Silverback/Netflix (cameraman Hugh Miller filming blue sharks off the coast of Cornwall, England)
Ben Macdonald/Silverback/Netflix (a drone flies over the Valle de la Luna in the Atacama desert, the driest place on Earth)
Evgeny Tabalykin (cameraman Kieran O'Donovan staking out wild boar in the Forests of Sikhote-Alin, Russia
Alex Voyer/Silverback/Netflix (researcher Oliver Scholey swimming on the surface holding his stills camera)

Our Amazing Planet (page 87, clockwise from top)
Sophie Lanfear/Silverback/Netflix (helicopter filming calving of Store Glacier, Greenland)
Gisle Sverdrup/Silverback/Netflix (cameraman Doug Anderson filming giant stingrays, Bimini, Bahamas)
Sophie Lanfear/Silverback/Netflix (whilst the crew stopped filming for lunch, a curious king penguin wants to know what this strange object is? After a good look and investigative peck, the penguin decides to leave the camera control deck alone.)
Huw Cordey/Silverback/Netflix (Matt Aeberhard filming orangutans in Suaq Belimbing, Leuser Ecosystem, Sumatra)